GARDENS *of* NAPLES

Elisabeth Blair MacDougall
Introductory Essay

Nicolas Sapieha
Photographs

M. T. Train/Scala Books
New York

DISTRIBUTED BY
Antique Collector's Club

WAPPINGER'S FALLS, NEW YORK   WOODBRIDGE, ENGLAND

We thank each owner of the gardens included in this book and the Directors of the historic sights for their interest, help and hospitality that made this book possible.

We also wish to thank The Naples NinetyNine Foundation, Anna Acampora, Giancarlo and Carla Gaetani, Raimonda Gaetani, Shirley Hazzard, Pietro Lezzi, and Anna Maria Palmer for their thoughtful and generous advice.

First Published in the United States of America in 1995 by M.T. Train/Scala Books, New York

Copyright © 1995 M.T.Train/Scala Books

Photographs copyright © Nicolas Sapieha

Introductory essay and Reggia at Caserta by Elisabeth Blair MacDougall

Additional text by M.T. Train

Design by Our Designs, Inc., New York

Color Separation by Sfera, Milano

Printed and Bound in Italy by Sfera, Milano

ISBN 0-935748-95-4

Table *of* Contents

GARDENS *of* NAPLES

Introduction

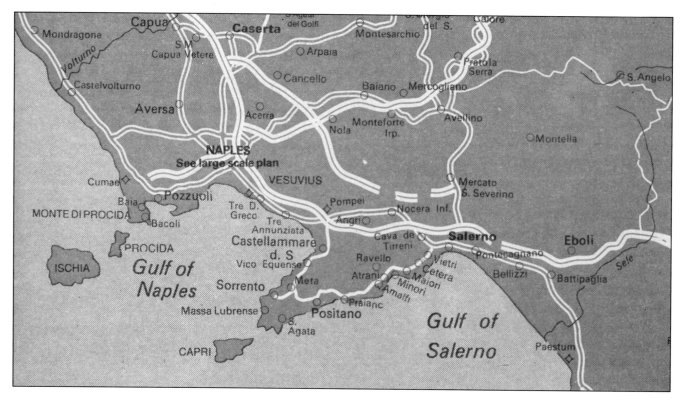

BACKGROUND

The great promontories that protect the bay of Naples provide shelter from all but the winds of Africa; the enclosed area provides ample anchorage for both shipping and war vessels. These physical characteristics have influenced the history of the Naples region since its origins. The bay has enticed waves of settlers and invaders throughout the centuries starting with Greek colonization of the islands and the mainland, continuing with the Roman invasion from the north, Byzantine expansion from the east followed by Arabic, Norman, Angevin, Aragonese, and Bourbon invasions or conquests. From the fall of Rome until the nineteenth century, Naples, much of Campania, Sicily, and the islands of the bay, Procida, Ischia and Capri, were ruled by foreigners. The area came under central Italian rule with the unification of the whole peninsula in 1860.

There is a remarkable continuity in the design, planting and appearance of the gardens and villas of this area over their two thousand year history, the result of the natural landscape and cultural traditions. Sites for villas are limited by the hilly of cliflike topography of the region which is determinant in their design. Only the flat stretch between Torre

del Greco and Castellammare di Stabia is suitable for large scale gardens and parks such as are found elsewhere in Italy. Most of the coastline of the Bay of Naples, and of the southern coast of its southern promontory is lined with cliffs. Thus villas and gardens were repeatedly rebuilt as the ownership of the choicest sites changed over the millennia. There are as many layers of occupation as there are multiple layers of lava in the vicinity of Mount Vesuvius.

The magnificent views of the bay and the ocean and the islands from the cliffs have been the chief determinant in the choice of sites for villa residences, in the creation of the multiple terrace levels and even the placement of trees and plants. Descending terraces providing views of the sea have been an essential part of the villa design in every period from the Romans to today, as we can see in views of the

**Posillipo,
Villa Carafa, engraving.**

4

Roman imperial Villa Jovis on Capri, the sixteenth-century Villa Carafa di Spina at Posillipo, or the eighteenth-century Villa Rufolo in Ravello, the early twentieth-century Villa Astor in Sorrento, La Mortella, Lady Walton's villa on Ischia. The nature of the topography is also responsible for design characteristics of villas and gardens in Posillipo and in the areas near or in Positano, Ravello and the Amalfi coast. Great expanses of gardens and parks, like those in northern Italy are found only in the area known in the eighteenth-century as the *Miglio d'Oro*.

The mild semi-tropical climate also plays a role in the story of these villas and gardens, while the volcanic activity in the whole region created an exceptionally fertile soil. The ocean moderates temperatures, and the protective shelter provided by the hills to the north make it possible to grow a wide variety of plants from many climates–dry climate succulents and tropical forest specimens flourish equally well, and both appear in gardens of all periods in addition to the rich native flora. There is an unusually wide selection of plants with a varied palette of colors. Romans imported plants from the colonies, crusaders in the Middle Ages and the explorers of the Renaissance brought back representative examples of near Eastern, American and oriental flora, and as knowledge of the more remote regions of the world has expanded, so has the plant material available.

Nineteenth-century botanic gardens, private as well as institutional, displayed a wide variety of plants, and the display of exotics continues to be an important feature in even the most recent gardens.

Continuity is also provided by the presence of Roman remains which have been the source of inspiration to later eras, both for the inclusion of surviving monuments within the garden (Roman Theater at Villa at Posillipo and by the display of architectural fragments and sculptures as an integral feature of garden decoration (Villa Astor in Sorrento, Villa De Gregorio di Sant'Elia on the *Miglio d'Oro*).

Variety provided by succeeding waves of invasions and conquests, while the lure of the favorable climate and magnificent scenery continues to attract foreigners to this day. Each brings something of their homeland–decorative details like the intermeshed moldings on the courtyard wall at Villa Rufolo, or planting styles, such as the typical English perennial borders at La Mortella, Villa Astor and Villa Cimbrone.

Design concepts have varied the most–at times gardens have been laid out with strictly axial and geometric plans, as in earliest park at Caserta or at the Palazzo Reale at Portici. In other periods, the informal and irregular style epitomized by the English gardens at Caserta and Capodimonte have dominated, to the point in many cases that earlier formal gardens were replaced with English style parks.

GREEK AND ROMAN GARDENS

During the period of Greek occupation, the coast between Mount Procida to the west and Paestum to the east was built up and Naples was found; the date is uncertain but probably before the Roman takeover in the fourth century B.C. Remains of the Greek civilization have almost disappeared with the notable exception of Paestum. Little is known about Greek gardens, but there is evidence that temple precincts were planted with shrubs and trees. It is highly likely that the temples at Paestum were surrounded by regularly spaced shrubs as was the Temple of Theseus in the Agora in Athens, and even cult figures, especially those associated with nature, were sometimes placed in a grove planted as a background to the statue and altar. Plato's Academy met in a grove by the river in Athens. Pleasure gardens, per se, appear at the residences of the Hellenistic rulers, but before that time simple wall fountains and probably potted plants were the only form of decoration for house courtyards in cities or near rural farm yards.

From the fourth century B.C. onward, Romans built villas in areas surrounding Naples, such as Posillipo, Baiae and Chiaia, or the Campi Flegrei, as well as along the coastal areas and on the slopes of Mount Vesuvius. Although, with the exception of Pompeii,

Capri, Villa Jovis.

only ruins have survived, paintings and descriptions provide a picture of the villas and their gardens, and the life lived in them. Imperial villas were gigantic complexes; Emperor Tiberius's Villa Jovis on Capri, or the great imperial villa at Baiae, or one believed to have belonged to Poppea, wife of the emperor Nero were built by the citizens of Pompeii and Naples, and tiny gardens and courtyards were a common feature in the towns.

The imperial villas usually consisted of a large number of loosely organized buildings connected by courtyards and corridors. At Tiberius's villa, built on the crest of Mount Tiberius in Capri, the buildings alone covered 7000 square meters, and the gardens, with grottoes, nymphaea, and fountains must have extended far beyond that in every direction. At the top, a long corridor opened on the panorama of the Bay of Naples to the north and east, and the mountainside on the eastern side descended in terraces 40 meters from top to bottom.

The most complete picture of Roman villa and town gardens can be found at Pompeii and Herculaneum. These towns, on the flanks of Mount Vesuvius, were founded by Oscans and Samites, and then conquered by the Romans in the fourth century B.C. From then on they developed the characteristic grid plans of Roman colonies. Both were busy economic centers, dealing in the products of the fertile countryside, and with industrial production of pottery, and metal works. Pompeii is a few miles inland from the coast, while Herculaneum was on the shore and was a busy port town. Mount Vesuvius, the still active volcano, had erupted several times during recorded history, but in 79 A.D. a disastrous eruption buried Pompeii in lapilli (small pieces of solidified lava) and slag six and seven meters deep. Herculaneum was buried in mud,

Pompeii, Impluvium at the House of Lucrezio Frontone.

ashes, pumice and some lava which solidified into an impervious cover, in some places 20 meters deep. Most of the inhabitants died but the buildings survived at least in part, with their contents preserved. Excavations have laid bare the closely packed town center with its stores, public buildings and homes, as well as the villas on the periphery and in the neighboring villages such as Boscotrecase.

Traditional Roman houses had an open courtyard with an impluvium, a pool or cistern to catch rainwater. By the end of the Republican era in many the open area was edged with colonnades, plants in pots were placed in the court, and often a statue or fountain was located in the center. The peristyle garden, as these were called, of the House of Vettii, although now restored with inappropriate and inaccurate plants, suggest the appearance of these gardens. The tradition of creating a garden with potted plants continues to this day as in Palazzo d'Avalos. Peristyle gardens were also built behind the house, usually with the triclinium opening onto them. They often had elaborate fountains, as well as statues and plants, including trees as in the House of the Faun.

FAR LEFT: **Pompeii, Peristilio garden at the House of the Vettii.**

LEFT: **Pompeii, Atrium at the House of the Faun.**

OPPOSITE RIGHT: **Pompeii, fresco of a *villa marittima*.**

OPPOSITE FAR RIGHT: **Stabia, fresco of a villa by the sea.**

The great monastic foundations outside the cities had herb and cloistered gardens within the conventual buildings as well as orchards and cultivated fields. The innermost cloister, a place set aside for meditation and prayer as well as for strolling, was frequently planted with ornamentals and had well houses; Cistercian's were particularly elaborate as they were required to wash before entering the refectory, see the well head in the Certosa of S. Martino.

Within the towns, monasteries and small gardens behind the homes existed side by side, and the eighteenth-century bird's eye view shows the urban pattern established in the middle ages and continued until recent times. The former great park of Castel Nuovo has long since disappeared. The castle was constructed by the Angevin King Charles II in the late thirteenth century but became famous for its decorations by painters like Giotto (no traces of these frescos remain), and for the sophistication of the court and for its great park during the reign of his successor, Robert. Contemporary descriptions and documents show that the park had many varieties of trees and shrubs, a number of walks and pavilions, one with a gilded wooden ceiling, a fountain with a gilded roof, and a collection of wild animals and cages of exotic birds.

Records are not clear on what plants and shrubs were in use during this period, but early herbals show that a wide range of ornamental plants were known, many of them used for medical and culinary purposes as well as for color and scent in the enclosed gardens. Plants were placed in raised beds–the fifteenth century Crescenzi manuscript show such beds being prepared under the supervision of the author of the treatise.

The Castel Nuovo was also the site of the first appearance in Naples of Renaissance art, the central Italian revival of the culture of ancient Rome and Greece. There Alfonso I, erected the famous triumphal arch with its classicizing architectural forms and sculpture to commemorate his entry into Naples in 1443.

In the 1490s, Alfonso II commissioned the Florentine architect, Giuliano da Maiano, to design a suburban villa, Poggio Reale, which introduced the Renaissance style of garden design to Naples. Formal and geometric beds were set alongside the swimming pool, while the four-towered residence was built around an open atrium. This villa, now

Poggio Reale, plan of Naples by Alessandro Baratta, 1670.

destroyed, started anew the fashion for suburban villas, and many more were built in this period. Alfonso II's court was notable for its humanist scholars and poets, many of whom celebrated their villas in poems. The treatise, *De Magnificentia*, written by one of Alfonso's courtiers, the poet and humanist, Giovanni Gioviano Pontano, evokes life at these villas:

Map of Reggia at Portici, by Duca di Noya, 1775.

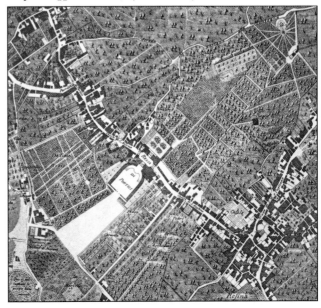

[The villa owner is] to have gardens in which to exercise by walking, or for banquets as the occasion demands. The gardens will have exotic plants and superb tress, very artfully and properly arranged. In them topiary work in myrtle, box, citrus and rosemary is most highly to be recommended....The gardens contribute wonderfully to the splendor of the villa, which is not rustic, but a magnificent *villa urbana*....

In addition to the luxurious villas of the nobility, many smaller suburban villas and gardens were built by the scholars and humanists at the court. Poets, such as Iacomo Sannazaro, celebrated these in verse, at poetry readings and symposia, held in the villas.

BAROQUE AND ROCOCO GARDENS

Many palaces were built in the urban center of Naples in the seventeenth and eighteenth centuries but they rarely had extensive grounds. Roof terraces supplied areas for promenades, views of city or sea, and their gardens supplemented or substituted for ground level courtyard plantings. Few have survived, but the terrace of the Palazzo Reale, now a museum and the seat of the *Biblioteca Nazionale*, retains its monumental appearance and attests to the role such areas played in the life of their owners. Outside the dense urban center, the steep rocky terrain limited garden sites to the descending terraces found throughout the region.

At the same time that the urban and suburban gardens were flourishing in and near Naples, the area on the flanks of Mount Vesuvius which had been reclaimed for agriculture during the late Middle Ages, royal and aristocratic families gradually began to convert the farms into villas, with pleasure gardens replacing the former farm lands. The process began in the sixteenth century but reached its apogee in the succeeding two centuries. The area near the sea was thickly built up with villas, particularly during the eighteenth century.

Seventeenth and early eighteenth-century garden design was based on long central axes and formal geometric parterres. Along the *Miglio d'Oro*, the coastal area between Naples and Torre del Greco, the villa buildings and their long allées were sited to take advantage of the sea view, but similar layouts were used everywhere that the terrain permitted. Vanvitelli's original design for the Reggia at Caserta, 28 kilometers northeast of Naples, although dating from the mid-eighteenth century, is characteristic of Baroque garden design. Just as the palace design emulated the palace erected by Louis XIV at Versailles, so the garden design had features similar to Versailles' gardens–a garden or park behind the palace led to a long central axis formed by a succession of water cascades interrupted by great pools with fountains. The axis terminates at the Cascade of Diana, 80 meters above the palace park.

A similar design was used at the Palazzo Reale on the coast at Portici. Built for King Charles, the first of the Bourbon rulers, who also commissioned the palace at Caserta. His building activities, especially at Portici, led to a great proliferation of villas built by the nobility, in which grandiose palaces were surrounded by extensive gardens. At first these followed the French Baroque style, but later in the eighteenth century, the less rigid curvilinear shapes and decorations of the rococo prevailed. Elaborate gardens with complicated designs, such as the Villa Vannucchi's concentric circles with the villa building in the center, became common. Buildings were ornamented with elaborate stuccoes, sometimes resembling the frosting on a wedding cake, and whimsical

Naples, A plan for Palazzo Reale by Antonio Niccolini (1772–1850).

OPPOSITE: **Naples, Palazzo di Tarsia, engraving by Domencio Antonio Vaccaro, 1739.**

fountains, follies and other garden structures festooned the grounds.

Majolica tiles became fashionable decorations in this period and examples could be intimate, as in the scattered rose petal design in a bedroom at the Parco dei Principi in Sorrento. In other cases, as in the Cloister of the Clarisse in the Convent of Sta. Chiara, tiles, which covered the surfaces of all the portico and pergola supports, as well as the benches, showed landscapes, rural scenes, mascarades and mythological stories.

Interest in botanical discoveries was high in this period; the importation of exotic varieties, *"un po d'ogni parte,"* as one author describes, was in vogue. Their display in gardens and glass houses was an important feature of many of the villas.

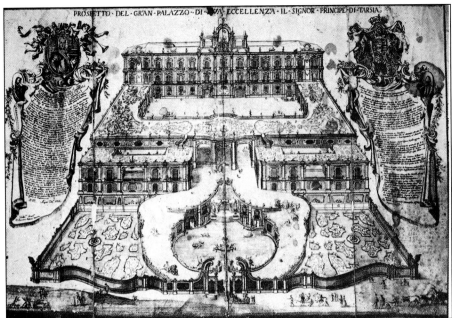

NINETEENTH AND TWENTIETH CENTURY GARDENS

The nineteenth century was a period of great upheaval in Naples and the surrounding region. Briefly ruled at the beginning of the century by Joseph Bonaparte, and Joachim Murat, Napoleon's brother and general, respectively, it was retaken by the Bourbons who ruled until Garibaldi made it his headquarters in the fight for the unification of Italy. Subsequently, Campania with Naples its capital, became a province of the unified country ruled by the Savoy king of Piedmont, the new nation's first monarch.

The changes in government were reflected in villa and garden styles. The French imported the neo-classical, or Empire style, and with it the fashion for Egyptian ornaments, both reflected in villa buildings and garden decorations. Interest in the display of ancient statues and architectural fragments both inside buildings and in the gardens was aroused by the ongoing excavations at Pompeii and Herculaneum. Hamilton and Nelson, English ambassadors and residents in Naples built villas that reflected the neo-classicism. A prime example of the style is the series of structures built on the several descending terraces of the Villa Rosebery in Posillipo, now an Italian Presidential possession. Recently restored, the structure's gleaming white façades with

classicizing ornaments, epitomize the restraint and sobriety of the new vogue as does the former residence, now museum at the Villa Pignatelli in Naples. Its garden is in the so-called English Garden style that replaced formal garden design at this time. The informal and picturesque layouts added to the Reggia at Caserta, and to the gardens of the royal palace at Capodimonte became *de rigeur* for villas large and small. Most of the Baroque and rococo gardens were destroyed, to be replaced with the sweeping open areas and scattered groves of the new approach to garden design, while romantic and exotic structures were scattered informally throughout the grounds.

The romantic movement of the mid-century brought interest in historical and exotic features. The Villa Rufolo in Ravello, which dates in part to the thirteenth century, was restored in the mid-nineteenth century by its Scottish owner to retain its Moorish Sicilian features and added new parts in the same style. Later in the century it became the vogue to divide the gardens into separate areas each of which had a different style, e.g. Moorish, Japanese, Roman, etc. This eclecticism parallel the styles of interior decoration in this period.

The nineteenth century also saw the development of botanical gardens created for the study of botany and as a display of plants of many different origins. While the first scientific gardens were started in Tuscany in the sixteenth century, they proliferated in the nineteenth century. The *Orto Botanico* in Naples was created by decree of Joseph Bonaparte in 1807, primarily for the study of agricultural and commercial plants. Later it evolved into a display collection of plants from all over the world. A similar history can be found in most of the botanical gardens of that era; the development of new techniques at this time for shipping live plants made displays possible that could not be created with the dried specimens or seeds formerly collected. Private owners also benefited from the new technology, and many villa gardens had specimens as exotic as those found in the botanical gardens.

As always the mild climate and rich soil provided ideal conditions for the adaptation of plants from other parts of the world.

The large scale villas and parks of the previous two centuries became too costly to construct and maintain after World War I and many have been abandoned, given over to institutions, as the Palazzo Reale, which has become the Botanic Garden of the Faculty of Agriculture of the University of Naples or converted into hotels, such as Le Sirenuse in Positano or the Parco dei Principi in Sorrento. In others the cycle from farm to pleasure grounds have been reversed, and orchards and vegetable plots have replaced the former English parks and exotic plantings.

Nevertheless, villa building has continued throughout the century, although in a much smaller scale. Elaborate planting designs are rare; the bedded out parterres at the Villa Rufolo are an exception to the rule. The keynote to the modern style is informality both in planting and in a way of life. In place of grandiose terraces sites are divided into series of "rooms" frequently with no visual link between them. Furnished with rustic or informal fur-

niture these outdoor spaces have none of the formality of earlier salons or dining rooms, but speak of a simpler more casual way of life.

Planting materials and style have become more varied and informal. Texture and color are important. Groups of plants of different texture, height, growth habit and variety of color are massed to create an overall effect. One might compare the result to the impressionistic style of painting. Specimen plants are not isolated but set off against contrasting backgrounds, while colored varieties are mixed together in scintillating combinations.

The distinction between a designed garden and untamed nature has dissolved, so that rocky cliffs like those at La Rondinaia in Ravello may have ornamental and colorful plants tucked into crevices or cascading down the face and rocks or other natural features are integrated into garden design. Fountains and pools emulate natural springs and ponds, and water trickles and drops rather than bursting out in great jets of water. The most formal design for water occurs in the ever-more popular swimming pools. Aroma is an element in design—strongly perfumed flowers and shrubs are used, or scented herbs planted throughout the garden.

Yet tradition continues to play a role. Tufa walls, bamboo screens and windbreaks, ancient fragments and many other features from the past are still in use. In the recent restored garden at the Villa Savarese in Sorrento the owner has constructed a pergola in the traditional Sorrentino form; lemon trees are trained over it just as ancient Romans would have done.

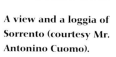

A view and a loggia of Sorrento (courtesy Mr. Antonino Cuomo).

REGGIA & GARDENS AT CASERTA

O ne of the most magnificent works executed during the Bourbon kingdom was the Palace and Gardens at Caserta begun by Luigi Vanvitelli in 1752.

Inspired by King Charles's passion for hunting, this royal monument and seat of government was built close to Naples amidst forests and fields.

Luigi Vanvitelli, plan for the gardens of Reggia at Caserta.

The two mile vista begins at the palace and ends in a superb water staircase. In the foreground the Fountain of the Dolphins, followed by a landing at the Fountain of Aeolos. From here another landing leads to a long pool filled by the water passing through seven rapids from the Fountain of Ceres. Another pool with twelve rapids flows down to the Fountain of Venus and Adonis. A flight of steps, borded by statues, reaches the basin also called the Fountain of Diana and Actaeon. The aqueduct descends from a grotto high up in the forest. On the right of the basin is the entrance to the English Garden. The entrance to the Castelluccia and the fish pond are closer to the palace on the left side.

The Royal Palace or Reggia at Caserta was started by Charles de Bourbon, king of Naples, between 1734 and 1759 with the design of Luigi Vanvitelli, the chief court architect. The enormous structure, one of the largest if not the largest in Europe at that time, occupies 4.5 hectares (11.25 acres). In the time honored custom of rulers with their monuments, it was intended not just to "keep up with" Versailles, but to outdo it. Successive generations of rulers have made many internal alterations since its completion but the exterior remains unaltered, a future predicted by an inscription on its corner stone: "This palace, this soil and Bourbon descendants will remain until this stone returns to heaven."

Both the palace and the park exemplify the changes in style that took place during the hundred years of their construction. On the interior, the eastern wing of the palace, finished and occupied in the 1780's, was decorated in the prevalent rococo style, while the western wing has neo-classical decorations. The original park was laid out like the great Baroque garden of Versailles–an axial design with long allées dividing the expanse into severely geometric parterres. In 1782 an "English Garden" was added to the east of the long central axis with informal wandering paths, a natural appearing lake, follies and natural groupings of trees and shrubs.

The most prominent feature of the original park is the long avenue that leads from the rear façade of the palace nearly two miles to the top of the hill. The aqueduct built to bring water more than 25 miles from nearby hills terminates there in a grotto. The tree lined avenue starts at the fountain of Margherita, and continues to the top of the hill, more than 150 meters higher than the level of the palace. In its center a series of cascades bring water from the hill, past a number of pools and fountains. The first pool, 475 meters (ca. 1300 feet) long; in an earlier period live dolphins were kept there to entertain the court and the royal children. There follows a series of pools and fountains, the latter with sculpture groups which depict dramatic scenes from Roman mythology. First is the fountain dedicated to Aeolos, the god of the winds, with 29 statues of various winds disposed on an artificial cliff. Next comes the pool and fountain of Ceres, goddess of the earth with statues of dolphins, tritons and personified rivers. Beyond and up the cascade is the fountain of Venus and Adonis, her ill-fated lover. The series culminates in the great fountain of Diana and Actaeon, the mortal who was destroyed by her hounds for the sin of spying on her bathing with her nymphs. The sculptures, executed by various Neapolitan sculptors in the

OPPOSITE: **From the Fountain of Ceres the two–mile water course descends amidst flower beds, groves of trees, fountains, statues, niches, steps and arches. The majestic palace appears in the far distance.**

One of the statues on the balustrade of the fountain Aeolos.

1770s and 1780s, are in the grandiose and highly move-
mented style of the late rococo, and the subject matter
drawn from Roman mythology, traditional for gardens since
the Roman era.

There seem to be no records of the planting of the park,
but one may imagine that the parterre closest to the palace
were bedded out with flowers changed by the season, and
with small topiary shrubs, as was done at Versailles. The
outer parterres were probably parterres de gazon, that is
planted with grass.

The English Garden, which was started in 1782 under the
supervision of the Englishman J. A. Graefer, represents the
newly fashionable landscape style, and is among the first of
this kind in the Naples area. Its winding paths conform to the
terrain, while apparently randomly placed statues evoke a
nostalgic and romantic mood. There are pretend ancient ruins
with truly ancient statues brought from Pompeii; a statue of a
bathing Venus kneels on a rock on a small island in the lake,
artificial cliffs, and even a statue of an ancient shepherd.

Trees of many varieties are planted in groups throughout
this area–pines, cedars of Lebanon, cypress, sycamores, and
many rare and exotic plants from other parts of the world. All
contribute to the romantic and evocative mood of this garden.

CASERTA

**OPPOSITE: After a long water
way flanked by mature
trees, a fountain featuring
the allegory of the love of
Venus and Adonis greets
the eye. The goddess on
her knees begs Adonis to
be prudent in his hunt.
This central couple is
surrounded by hordes of
nymphs and putti climbing
the edges of the rocks, their
bodies posed to suggest the
buffeting effect of waters.
Below, the boar who will
gore Adonis awaits his
prey. The fountain was
designed and built by
Gaetano Salomone
between the years 1770–80.**

**The fountain of Aeolos or the Winds: Constructed in the shape of a large
horseshoe with arches at the bottom and statues above. The bas-reliefs on
the façade are inspired by the Iliad and the Aeneid. They depict the wedding
of Thetis and Peleos, the judgment of Paris, Jove and the Three Goddesses,
and the wedding of Paris. Together they serve as prologue for of the main
fountain group that illustrates Juno compelling Aeolos to wreak havoc on
Aeneas and the Trojans. On the balustrade are various sculpted slaves, some
shackled in pairs, while in the middle of the basin winged nymphs cavort.**

CASERTA

The Fountain of Diana and Actaeon: On the right Diana is attended by her nymphs. On the left, as punishment for spying on the divine goddess in her bath, Actaeon is set upon by his hounds and transformed into a stag. The sculptures are by Paolo Persico, Angelo Brunelli and Pietro Solari. The Caroline aqueduct, designed by Carlo Vanvitelli, terminates in a quiet pool in the back of this group of sculptures. Started in 1753 and considered an engineering triumph, this aqueduct supplies the entire garden with water from sources as distant as thirty-two miles.

On the left side of the main garden, Ferdinand IV had Vanvitelli design the Castelluccia, a small octagonal building with a cylindrical tower, conceived as an amusement place for the young Bourbon princes and their friends. Vanvitelli decorated the site with artificial grottoes and a Chinese Pavilion.

An immense fish-pond with a central island was added at the same time.

VILLA AT POSILLIPO
PREVIOUS PAGE: A walk shaded by pines crowns the Roman theatre, with its rising rows of stone steps.

A tufa brick wall secures the vegetation desending the hill.

OPPOSITE: A rampant cactus stands in front of a vista of the Posillipo coast.

VILLA ON THE HILL

Nestled between the densely populated coastline and the Vomero, another concentration of buildings higher up on the hill, lies a secluded stretch of greenery. Scattered here and there within this area are Naples's hillside villas, each with a spacious garden looking out upon the bay and Vesuvius beyond. Each of them boasts its own particular collection of artistic and botanical treasures.

Detail of a brick staircase, enhanced by tiles, and accented with large decorative stone planters teeming with geraniums.

OPPOSITE: The garden entrance from the villa boasts its original white wrought–iron canopy framed by a bougainvillea and climbing ivy. A Baroque wall with a stone fountain base borders a path. Brick walk–ways cross the green lawn of this unusually large garden in the urban center.

A HILLSIDE VILLA
A bower of rhododendron rises over the balustrade.

A huge magnolia tree stands below the balustrade while pine trees shade the lawn of this multileveled garden.

OPPOSITE: A tempietto in the garden covered by climbers.

View from the Hillside Villa.

CLOISTER
STA. CHIARA

This colorful tile, part of a bench in the cloister, shows a typical *hortus inclusus*: raised flowers along with utilitarian plantings of herbs and vegtables. The atmosphere of tranquility and seclusion created by these gardens is often furthered by a central round fountain, the waters of which would have typically been used for watering and washing.

After having been badly bombed during World War II, this early fourteenth–century church was reconstructed in the spirit of its Gothic simplicity.

Yellow, green and blue are the dominant colors in the Cloister of the Clarisse, one of the most beloved and remarkable cloisters in Naples. It was transformed into a refined garden by Domenico A. Vaccaro in 1742. Planted with seasonal flowers, camellia, and fruit trees, the court is divided by four large pathways. Their walls and benches are completely covered with glazed Capodimonte majolica tiles by Giuseppe and Donato Massa. These depict life in Naples, at sea and in the monastery, along with rural and mythological scenes, carnival trophies, and parades. Magnificent octagonal columns, also covered with tiles with floral motifs, hold thick vines and wisteria that shade the walks and benches.

CLOISTER STA. CHIARA
OPPOSITE: A general view of the cloister's majolica–tiled columns which support a trellis of blooming wisteria.

Detail of an octagonal pillar and bench decorated with eighteenth–century tiles. In the background a flowering camellia.

CERTOSA OF S. MARTINO

Situated above the austere castle of Sant'Elmo, the Certosa of S. Martino was built by the Angiovins in 1325. It is now a famous repository of works depicting the history of Naples. The collection includes sections on navigation, rare maps, and paintings from the school of Posillipo, as well as period costumes. It is also much visited for its magnificent Nativity scene known as *Cucinello*.

The Grand Cloister was designed by Giovanni Antonio Dosio at the end of the sixteenth century. Cosimo Fanzago, architect and sculptor, added one level to the courtyard and completed the decoration in 1623. Each side is lined with sixteen columns, a central well is surrounded by fruit trees, and in the past the green areas were planted with flowers and herbs. A small cemetery with skulls is also enclosed in the cloister. Within the immense Certosa and its museum an intimate garden with olive trees, pergolati and vines is still kept and cherished.

The Grand Cloister, a view of the cemetary and on the opposite page the well with a camellia tree in the background.

PALAZZO
D'AVALOS

Town-gardens, of which this is an example, were usually hidden from public view by high walls. As early as the fourteenth century, prosperous town citizens took to adding back-yard gardens onto their residences. Among the typical elements of these informal outdoor living spaces were fountains, flower beds, statues, and perhaps a pergola-shaded stone table with benches. Ornamental terracotta flower pots containing laurel, clipped bushes, or orange and lemon trees, might also be included.

OPPOSITE: The garden entrance of the sixteenth-century palace showing an ancient urn in its niche. A large camellia tree proudly displays its red blooms.

In the vine-covered loggia different plants grow in pots and a clivia thrives in a disused fountain.

This lovely flower, indisputable queen of the gardens of Naples, first arrived in Italy at the Reggia at Caserta, presumably brought as a gift of love from Admiral Nelson to the enchanting Lady Emma Hamilton. The flower had originally been brought to Europe from China and Japan.

Tender, elegant and sensual, the camellia is described by Proust as "the flower of the soul" and Dumas fils and Verdi likewise immortalized it in *La Dame aux Camelia* and *La Traviata*.

The camellia found its ideal home in the gardens of the Vesuvian eighteenth century villas, between the oaks and citrus groves where shade, humidity and sunlight occur in perfect combination, as well as in the well shaded gardens in town. These beautiful flowers, planted in groves, allées, bordering pipero benches and encircling stone balustrades, bloom regularly every winter. Pink, white, red, and variegated colors have been planted, and varieties range from single and double growths to clusters.

Camellia flowers fade as soon as they are plucked, so to prolong the beauty of this symbolic flower when picked, eighteenth-century aristocrats used to preserve the camellia in a mixture of sugar and flavorings. These candied flowers were part of the decoration of the famous Neapolitan sweets and have adorned gala tables from past days up to the present.

VILLA PIGNATELLI

Bought in 1841 by the Rothschilds, Villa Pignaltelli was built by Pietro Valente for Ferdinand Acton in 1820 and was at that time the center of the intellectual and fashionable life of the city. The garden, designed by Bechi, is particularly precious to the city as it is the only one left along the Riviera. The neo–classic palace with its Doric columns is now a museum surrounded by a lush garden. A pavilion containing a museum of nineteenth and twentieth century coaches surrounded by palms and pines is also part of the Villa Pignatelli.

PALAZZO REALE

The immense terrace garden, one of the largest in the world, stretches the entire length of the building. A monumental marble table topped with a planter serves as the focal point of the garden, its position accentuated by the checkered marble pavement. Vine–covered trellises are placed at either end of the huge table. Each of these allées is built in segments and divided by decorative fountains.

The Royal Palace was conceived by Fontana in the beginning of the seventeenth century during the Spanish domination. The great architect Vanvitelli enlarged it about 140 years later while it was the residence of the Bourbon kings. Later it housed Murat and Caroline Bonaparte. This magnificent palace is not only an important museum, but is known as well for its National Library, which preserves several unique collections of ancient volumes.

View towards the façade and the terrace of the Royal Palace.

LA FLORIDIANA

Situated on the Vomero, this delightful villa is surrounded by an extraordinary countryside featuring a panorama of Naples with Capri in the distance. The villa's name derives from Donna Lucia, daughter of the Duke of Floridia, morganic wife of Ferdinand IV of the Two Sicilies. Their marriage took place in Palermo on November 27, 1814, and the date is commemorated by a sundial on the façade of the villa.

"La Floridiana" is built on a rectangular plan, with two wings perpendicular to the central structure. The elegant neo–classic façade is a wonderful example of the work of Antonio Niccolini, whom Ferdinand IV entrusted with the construction of the villa.

Niccolini also undertook the placement and design of the architectural elements in the park. These consist of a small circular temple, an open–air theatre, a greenhouse for exotic

From the front of the villa one can enjoy one of the most spectacular panoramas of the city, featuring the gulf and the island of Capri. From the round fountain at the center of the terrace, walks spread out to different parts of the garden and the park.

OPPOSITE: The façade of the Villa, seen from the round fountain.

plants, a labyrinth, belvederes, and grottoes with bears, lions and a tiger cage.

The botanical elements of the garden were supervised by the German botanist Dehenhardt, director of the Botanical Gardens of Naples, who previously won acclaim for his designs for the park at Capodimonte. The park "La Floridiana" was based entirely on the system of the English Garden. Characteristic of this system are its complete lack of symmetry, with paths winding playfully through picturesque scenery.

In 1919 "La Floridiana" was acquired by the State and became The National Museum of Porcelain Duca di Martina, who in 1931 donated his world famous collection of porcelain and other objects of art to the city of Naples. This donation enriched the collection of the museum and made it one of the most important porcelain museums in the world. It is especially renowned for its collection of Sèvres, Chinese and Japanese exports, and silver.

With its beautifully maintained walks and magnificent views, "La Floridiana" offers the people of Naples a delightful respite. It is one of the city's most frequented and loved parks.

LA FLORIDIANA
OPPOSITE: The circular
temple, overlooking the
gulf, was also built by
Antonio Niccolini for King
Ferdinand IV.

An impressive variety of trees grows in the park including pine,
oak, elm, plane, linden, magnolia, cedar, cypress, and palms of
many kinds. In the spring its world-famous camellias burst in a
multitude of colors, while the statues and fountains scattered along
the intervining paths of the English park boast rhododendron, field
flowers and climbers.

LA FLORIDIANA
Niches with sculptures in the English park.

CAPODIMONTE

Sanfelice designed the five main allées radiating from the Porta di Mezzo
which is enclosed by a wrought iron gate. Surrounding the palace is the famous
English Garden added by F. Dehenhardt, one of the first of these in Naples.

The magnifcent yet austere Royal Palace and the Park of Capodimonte were commissioned by Charles of Bourbon. The Palace, which holds the art collection given to him by his mother Elisabetta Farnese, was designed by Giovanni A. Medrano in 1734. Today the museum hosts a variety of traveling exhibits from around the world.

View from Capodimonte, as painted by Alexander H. Dunouy (1757–1841).

Ville Vesuviane–
Miglio d'Oro

Vesuvius, at one time covered with forests and saturated with the intense perfume of yellow Mediterranean broom, serves as a natural centerpiece for the *Miglio d'Oro*, the famous stretch of coast-line extending from Naples to Torre del Greco. This area, completely destroyed by the eruption of 1631, became popular as a site for villas in the eighteenth century.

The enchanting beauty of this coast bewitched the Bourbon King Charles, who with Queen Maria Amalia Cristina of Saxony built the impressive Palazzo Reale at Portici. Members of the court soon followed the royal example and built neighboring residences, where gardens of unequaled imagination and richness were created to accompany them. The excavations of Pompeii and Herculaneum had also just begun and inspired the nobility to integrate themes from the new discoveries in their villas and gardens.

World-famous architects like Vanvitelli, Canevari, and Giofreddo lavished attention on the design and construction of these elaborately planned gardens. Allées, walks, vistas, follies, glorias, pergolas, fountains, pools and statuary were used to create Arcadias. Even today, one can imagine the *douceur de vie* exemplified by the villas of the *Miglio d'Oro*. Pastoral entertainments, balls, picnics, hunts, concerts, and countless intrigues were used to pass the time by the aristocrats of the period. Illustrious visitors, including Byron and Goethe, have left written testimony of the splendor of the Bourbon court and beauty of the *Miglio d'Oro*.

Architecturally, some villas were isolated within their surrounding parks and gardens, with long allées leading from villa to entrance gate. Others had façades directly on the streets and access to the gardens was obtained through a series of terraces and flights of stairs. In a third variety the gardens were sited on one side of the villa. Whatever the design of the villas themselves, a large straight allée leading towards the sea, and the omnipresent Vesuvius towering on the east, were constant motifs. The gardens were planted in such a way that Vesuvius was always visible above the tree-tops, and the glimmering sea visible on the opposite side. Tea houses and temples were situated on these walkways, and offered diverting places to rest and enjoy the view of the Mediterranean.

These jewels testify to the illustrious past of the *Miglio d'Oro*, and recall the prosperous and influential Kingdom of Naples. In 1839 the building of the Naples–Portici new road bisected the countryside and thus began the slow decline of the area. Over the years the palaces, villas and surrounding gardens have been forgotten and left to deteriorate in silence. In 1971 the *Ente per le Ville Vesuviane* was created in order to retrieve and enhance the patrician eighteenth century villas and gardens. Some have already been restored and successfully readapted.

The blackness and solidity of the tufa is only cut out with great difficulty. Tufa bricks are used to retain a flow of solidified lava into which steps are cut.

A view of Vesuvius from the terrace of one of the remaining Vesuvian villas which still stand amidst its protective deep woods.

VILLA DE GREGORIO DI SANT' ELIA

One of the most representative and best kept of the Vesuvian villas, the Villa de Gregorio di S. Elia is a treasure of Naples's eighteenth-century architectural heritage. The ample entrance courtyard is surrounded by curved and rectangular niches housing marble statues. The courtyard leads to the reception room which, in turn, opens onto the garden. In 1866 Nicola Breglio enlarged and elaborated upon the original decorations of the villa respecting the design of the façade by L. Vanvitelli.

The garden as laid out is representative of the original concept of eighteenth-century gardens with an open view on an axis, surrounded by camellia trees, leading to flights of stairs ascending to leafy woods planted on a knoll. On the right serpentine walks traverse the English Garden with its follies, ponds and bridges. In front of the park is the Italian garden, complete with greenhouse and swimming pool. Though at one time they lavishly dotted the garden, today only a few statues remain visible between benches and other garden ornaments.

OPPOSITE: At the end of the lush garden a staircase rises to the park beyond. Water spouts from a mask in a baroque fountain where tall oaks shelter the perennial beds and surrounding ivy. Plantings of yucca and cactus can be seen in the background.

An overview of a section of the villa showing the swimming pool and part of the park, including oaks, pines, and magnolias.

VILLA DE GREGORIO
View from the terrace of the villa, showing the greensward surrounded by camellia trees. A nineteenth–century circular stone fountain is visible in front of a flight of stairs leading to the park in the back.

OPPOSITE: **A Baroque eighteenth–century stone bench is crowned by a classical terracotta bust and bordered by agapan–thus. A beautiful mimosa completes the scene.**

66

The evocative *Belle Epoque* greenhouse in cast–iron is still active and remains one of the focal points of the villa. Behind it extends the English Garden.

OPPOSITE: A charming arched stone bridge juts over the stream in the English Garden. Ivy creeps along the ground and among the rocks.

VILLA PROTA

The architect Antonio Vaccaro decorated the oldest parts of this structure in its present theatrical style, yellow stucco with contrasting white appliques. The result is a virtual encyclopedia of Neapolitan rococo at its most vivacious and exuberant.

The approach to the villa is bordered by scalloped rococo stucco walls decorated with classical terra-cotta urns planted with agave Desilirium.

A spray of mimosa.

Detail of the finials surmounting the archway which connects the two sections of the villa.

OPPOSITE: The villa can be reached from the sea by this long walkway bordered on one side by an orange grove. Beyond it, the leafy English Garden can be seen in the distance.

Palazzo Reale
at Portici

Maria Amalia Cristina of Saxony left Dresden in 1738 to marry Charles of Bourbon, King of Naples. She brought with her the memory of some beautiful statues excavated from the area of Vesuvius, and inspired by these works of art and enchanted by the country about Portici, decided to build a royal residence there; in spite of the suggestion that it was to near Vesuvius. King Charles remarked "God, the immaculate Virgin and S. Gennaro will protect us." Medrano and Canevari were selected as the initial architects for the project with Vanvitelli and F. Fuga collaborating later on. The edifice contains an octagonal royal chapel that was at one time a theatre, monumental flights of stairs, elaborate rooms adorned with marble and semi-precious stones, and numerous archaeological art objects. Used primarily as a summer residence for the king and his queen, Palazzo Reale

OPPOSITE: **Overview of the garden showing the stairway joining it to the courtyard of the palace. The stone fountain serves as the centerpoint, from which a series of garden walks radiate. From here, the traditional Italian use of greenery can be admired, with added interest inspired by the plantings of rare tropical plants.**

View of the center fountain, with its stone mermaids and mermen, surrounded by papyrus.

**Details of a large mosaic
originally made for the
private garden,
depicting a red jar, a
yellow urn and a border
decoration of red
berries and leaves.**

at Portici soon became a focal point for the region. Many nobles built villas in the area in order to be close to the monarch and enjoy the honors, benefits and amusements that came with such association.

The superb park and the garden were designed by Francesco Geri and later enlarged during the reign of Ferdinand IV. Both are embellished by many archaeological treasures from the area, as well as by fountains, kiosks, fish-ponds, and other traditional garden elements. Together, these elements make this garden and park the most magnificent of the *Miglio d'Oro*.

At Portici, in his palace, King Charles opened a museum for the antiquities of Herculaneum, and an academy was founded for the study of the history of these remarkable objects.

PORTICI
**Tall camellia trees scatter
their scarlet flowers on an
ancient fountain protected
by a classical figure.**

An imposing ornamental entrance crowned with urns serves as an entry to the park from the garden.

A fern frond extends above the fishpond.

VILLA CAMPOLIETO

This splendid eighteenth–century edifice has been lovingly restored and is one of the finest examples of the work by the *Ente per le Ville Vesuviane*. Designed by Giofredo, Giustiniani, and Vanvitelli, its elegant courtyard and impressive interior have found new life as the centerpiece for the Ente's extensive restoration projects. Concerts, opera, conferences, and art exhibitions draw many visitors to the villa, who can also enjoy its incomparable views of the sea.

The entrance to the villa incorporates an italianate garden with clipped hedges and multi-colored flowers planted in permanent flower-beds. The large atrium is in the form of a Greek cross. A magnificent flight of stairs, similar to the famous stairway at Caserta, curves its way to the piano nobile and leads to a splendid reception room covered by a spacious central dome.

The exterior portico consists of a large yet refined and intimate elliptical court surrounded by an arched covered walkway. To provide relief from the intense summer sun, a delightfully cool sunken garden was incorporated in the villa's design, and placed at the foot of the wide stairway descending from the elliptical court.

OPPOSITE: A restored fresco representing the villa in one of the many beautiful rooms of Campolieto shows the approach from the sea in earlier times.

View from the lawn towards the villa. The impressive open rotunda, reached by massive double staircases, houses a terrace boasting matchless views of the fields, parks and sea beyond.

CAMPOLIETO
Overview of the terrace
encircled by a colonnade,
with the sea beyond. This
vista is typical of Vesuvian
villas, which are always
oriented to the sea. A park
by the beach can be seen
on the left behind a
tapestry of yellow field
flowers. Below the
colonnade, the sunken
palm garden is visible.

CAPRI & ISCHIA

Both islands protect the entrance to the Gulf of Naples and are famous for their mild year–round climate. Their rich Mediterranean flora and dramatically varied terrain and scenery have won the islands high praise since Roman times. Evidence of the islands' strong seafaring tradition can still be found in the many narrow streets of the villages and their small houses. Whitewashed walls and flat roofs are covered with luxuriant vines and flowers. Grape vines, along with still more flowers, grow among the loggias, while tall palms and cypress rise here and there into the sky.

Capri, from its dazzling highlands to its wave–carved grottoes and sheer limestone cliffs, has always been loved and cherished and much deserves its popular name "the pearl of the sea". Tiberius created twelve imperial villas on the island, each with gardens containing splendid collections of statues and ornamental objects.

Ischia, the largest of the Phlegean islands, was originally connected with the mainland and is of volcanic origin. The island is known for its wonderfully diverse shoreline of cliffs, stupendous beaches and bays, and has also been famous for centuries for its thermal springs.

CAPRI

A typical pergola
overlooking the sea
towards Sorrento.

Lantana and bougainvillea
mix against a sun drenched
wall.

OPPOSITE: A Roman bust has
been placed on a trunk of a
tree in an entrance hall.

CAPRI

OPPOSITE: **detail of the circular temple at Villa Fersen.**

An intimate corner with a pink geranium growing along a stone bench.

CAPRI

From the top of the island, on the way to Villa Jovis, a view on a garden with cypress, pines and a lemon grove.

OPPOSITE: **one of the remains of the garden walls at Villa Damacuta with the ground covered by spring flora.**

A trumpet plant in bloom against cypress trees.

VILLA JOVIS

The largest and best preserved of Emperor Tiberius's imperial villas, Villa Jovis survives today as an extensive series of ruins atop a large and commanding hill. Laid out on several levels, the villa functioned as a fortress in the time of its use, and was further protected by forests which stretched out beyond its gardens. Tiberius spent the last seven years of his life on Capri, and brought the center of Roman power there before his death in 37 A.D.

A view of the famous "Tiberius's jump" marked by a yellow broom; a three hundred meter precipice from which, according to legend, the emperor made his enemies jump into the sea.

VILLA S. MICHELE

Detail of the pergola.

"Open to the sun, to the wind, to the voice of the sea as a Greek temple, and light, light, light everywhere." Thus said Axel Munthe, the Swedish doctor and writer the villa he built in Anacapri on a promontory at the foot of Mount Solaro in 1896.

The land bought for this purpose was made up of a vineyard with a farmer's house at its center; Munthe also bought the ruins of the chapel of S. Michele from which the villa's name comes.

During the construction, Roman ruins were found that are thought to have been part of one of Tiberius's twelve imperial villas. Remains of the excavations can still be seen in the garden: a wall with *opus reticulatum*, the ruins of a bedroom with mosaic floor, and some traces of colored murals.

The garden's most attractive feature, however, is its splendid location. A long pergola on top of the sea, full of roses, honeysuckle, and wisteria, opens onto a splendid view stretching from the island of Ponza all the way along the coast to Calabria. This pergola is joined to the villa by a sculpture court where Tiberius and Germanico's heads stand out. The statue of Artemis, the goddess of the hunt, also stands out, thanks to the silver eyes that Munthe added to it. The other end of the pergola joins an apse–shaped belvedere, from which a narrow staircase leads to the

OPPOSITE: The pergola with pebble floor is covered by vines.

chapel. Beyond this, a large terrace dominates the view of Anacapri.

On the balustrade of this terrace, the famous red granite sphinx looks over the blue Mediterranean sea. From the chapel a long cypress allée begins, from which paths lead to small meadows surrounded by mixed bushes and flowers which lend perennial color. Borders of cineraria, violets, myosotis, hyacinth, petunia, cyclamen, along with large groups of strelitzia, calla lily, geranium, azalea and hydrangea are also present. Forsythia, camellia, oleander, hibiscus, magnolia, cassia, and jasmine bushes mix with yucca, cycad, acanthus, and agave.

VILLA S. MICHELE
The sculpture garden. The statue of Artemis can be seen on the far right side behind Tiberius's head.

OPPOSITE: **The terrace with its spiral columns and sphinx commanding the view over the sea.**

ISCHIA
LA MORTELLA

According to legend the volcanic island of Ischia, the largest in the Bay of Naples, rose from the sea in 2200 B.C. after the mainland was shaken by a sequence of volcanic eruptions. It is the site of the earliest Greek colony in Italy, settled in 775 B.C., which functioned as a trading post for iron that was then shipped back to Greece.

After spending many years visiting this lovely island with its fishing villages, vineyards and charming pastel houses, the distinguished English composer Sir William Walton and his young wife Susana found a congenial parcel of land facing the sunset and covered with myrtle, from which the house got its name. At the time they bought it the property was covered with immense boulders, hard anthracite, dying chestnut trees, and holm oaks. In 1956 the Waltons asked their friend, the eminent English landscape architect Russell Page, to help them create a garden in this difficult terrain. He drew up a detailed plan which foresaw ten years of work. Stairways and paths were carved into the volcanic rock, and countless stones and boulders were moved. In spite of the many hot mineral springs, drinking water was unavailable on the island, so large underground cisterns were constructed as well. Many of the trees, plants, and flowers the Waltons had planted had already taken hold, and the house had been partially built into the rocky landscape, when Russell Page was invited to visit the gardens again. Water was now available on the island and Page was inspired by this to add an irrigation channel with melodious fountains accentuating the L-shape of the garden. An elliptical pond with three small islands formed from native boulders was also added thanks to the new supply of water.

OPPOSITE: View of the pool showing papyrus and lotus, large ferns, clusters of carnations bordering a flight of stairs, palms, and a pathway. Walks paved with rocks hewn from stone taken from Vesuvius radiate to different parts of the garden.

Detail of a stone head surrounded by verdant ivy.

96

Sir William traveled throughout the world for concert appearances, and used these opportunities to collect and bring back samples of rare plants for his garden. Friends and botanical gardens from all over the world also supplied seeds and plants to be added to the Walton's varied collection. Lady Susana, born in Buenos Aires, has taken particular interest in importing indigenous South American plants to La Mortella. The garden was at first planted with jacaranda, magnolia, judas trees, chorisia, and flowering eucalyptus. These were followed by hemerocallis, Japanese quinces, hibiscus, and many kinds of sub-tropical ferns and spiky plants. Hedges of local bay trees were planted for protection from the winds.

Constant vigilance is required to keep the garden up to the exacting standards of its owners. For example, Ischia's climate is so felicitous for climbing plants that special care must be taken so that the boulders are not completely encroached upon by ivy and creepers. The pond, in turn, is always in danger of becoming too crowded with papyrus, lotus, water lilies, and other aquatic plants.

Camellia, flowering from October to April, are the highlight of La Mortella, and their multi-colored blooms are visible throughout the property. They are intermixed with less extravagantly colored flowers, creating an atmosphere of tranquility and refined contemplation.

The house and garden together form the William Walton Foundation, which in 1985 opened its gardens to the public. In addition to its famous collection of Mediterranean tropical plants, the Foundation is also known for hosting talanted musicians and giving them the opportunity to study with world–famous artists. The Foundation also presents many concerts and dance performances.

LA MORTELLA
A trunk of Chorisia speciosa. This southern species is characterized by its prominent spikes. It is one of many plants imported by Lady Walton.

OPPOSITE: **View from the balcony of the house looking out toward Forio featuring a portion of La Mortella's huge variety of plants, including agave, pines, and palms.**

FOLLOWING PAGE: **The crocodile cascade is one of the fanciful destinations for walks in the new garden.**

LA MORTELLA

OPPOSITE: The irrigation channel, designed by Russell Page, forms an axis in the garden and is connected by two fountains.

CLOCKWISE FROM RIGHT: One variety of white aquileia to be found in the garden.

A beautiful calla lily framed by green leaves.

Papyrus growing by the edge of the lily pond.

OPPOSITE: **This rustic stone pyramid surmounting a rock was chosen by Sir William as his final resting place. The rock occupies a beautiful spot overlooking the port of Forio with Mount Epomeo, the highest point on Ischia, rising behind it.**

An amphora decorates garden steps.

The plaque reads:

WILLIAM WALTON O.M.
1902 ~ 1983
SING A SONG OF PRAISE
BELOVED AND REVERED MASTER
THIS ROCK HOLDS HIS ASHES
THE GARDEN HE SURVEYS
RUSSELL PAGE DESIGNED
TOGETHER WE HAPPILY
BROUGHT IT TO LIFE
SUSANA

'ALL BLISS CONSISTS
IN THIS
TO DO AS ADAM DID.'
TRAHERNE 1637 ~ 1674

A view of Sorrento, lithograph, 1814. (courtesy Mr. Antonino Cuomo).

THE SORRENTO PENINSULA

The drive to Sorrento from Naples is one of the finest in the world, passing through lovely valleys and promontories with magnificent views of the bay, its shores, and the islands.

Vineyards, olive plantations, and groves of oranges and lemons are sheltered from the winds by its surrounding mountains. Sorrento is built on three tree-filled ravines. Narrow flight of steps, sometimes cut directly into the rocks, descend steeply from the town down to the sea mixed all along the way with luxuriant vegetation.

Sorrento derives from the Latin *Sorrentum*, a name connected to a cult centering around the Sirens encountered by Ulysses on his voyages. Given the area's seductive atmosphere, the name is a most fitting one. The gardens spread over the whole peninsula vary in style and size: some are small, intimate, sunny Sorrentino gardens filled with local flowers and fruit trees; others are large English Gardens that include many imported plants. Some are terraced gardens descending to the sea, and some are working gardens with groves of citrus fruit and vegetables. All are deeply loved and carefully maintained by their owners.

PARCO DEI PRINCIPI

OPPOSITE: A magnificent allée of Washingtonia leads from one of the hotel buildings to the swan pond. Beyond, two Nolina brevifolia stand by the entrance to one of the parks smaller shaded paths.

A detail of the swan pond with a huge arum growing in its center and the Nolina brevifolia in full bloom in the background.

The magnificent Villa Gorchakow, formerly known as Villa di Poggio Siracusa, was built in 1792 by the Count of Syracuse, Leopoldo of Bourbon, cousin of Ferdinand IV the King of Naples. After the Bourbons fled the kingdom upon Garibaldi's arrival, this magnificent villa, perched on a high promontory overlooking the sea, passed through several hands. In 1885 the villa was acquired by Prince Costantino Gorchakow, cousin of the Romanovs. Constantine in turn gave it to his daughter Elena.

The Gorchakows loved the villa and its environs, and gave new life to the property, so long uninhabited and neglected. A veritable Almanach de Gotha was invited for the opening of the villa in the spring of 1893. Among the esteemed guests were: Alix of Hesse, future Empress of Russia; Princess Maude, future Queen of Norway; the Duke of York, the future King George V of England; the Princess of Anhalt–Baden, and Queen Sophia accompanied the Princess of Sweden.

The yellow stucco neo–Renaissance villa is enlivened by white trim and decorated with heraldic devices. Many marble terraces stretch along the cliffs. The huge halls of the villa saw many glamorous balls and concerts. Its floors are decorated with tiles imitating carpet designs. Most of the villa has remained as it was at the end of the eighteenth century. Not far from the villa, in a spot that enjoys the same breathtaking view, the new owners have built a modern hotel with a private beach, swimming pool, and all the required twentieth–century conveniences. The design is by the renowned architect Gió Ponti.

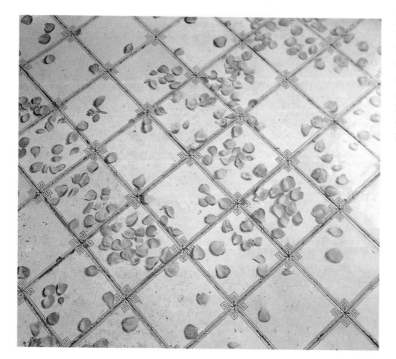

Rose petals on white tiles from Princess Gorchakow's bedroom. Legend has it the Princess had the tiles designed to match the petals of the roses outside her window, allowing her to imagine they had just blown in on the wind.

A bust on a pedestal against the wall of the villa is shaded by a wisteria.

BELOW: A view of the cornice of the villa Gorchakow.

The park has been well cared for by all the owners of the villa, starting with Count Leopoldo who transformed ordinary farmland into a joyous garden of Eden by transplanting and importing many varieties of plants, especially rare palm trees, that were interspersed with local vegetation. The park is now recognized as a botanical treasure and as inspiration for nature lovers.

Entering the park, the visitor is greeted by an apparent jungle of palms and greenery. In fact, well-laid out paths and walks lead throughout the property, allowing visitors to enjoy this tranquil oasis. A small circular temple, dedicated to Venus, commemorates the spot in the park where the first rare plants were cultivated. A pond for swans embellishes the park and leads to a bridge said to be the favorite of Desirée, first love of Napoleon.

The park is laid out in such a way that all its paths lead, as if drawn magnetically, to the high cliffs which drop precipitously to the beautiful azure sea below.

PARCO DEI PRINCIPI

OPPOSITE: A sample of one of the few remaining Jubaea spectabilis. This palm was named in honor of Juba II, king of Mauritania, who died in 25 B.C. and was a great student of nature. The stem of this palm can reach five meters in circumference and 15 to 20 meters in height. It bears bright yellow fruits resembling small coconuts.

The foliage of different palm trees intermingle, keeping the area pleasantly cool. An araucaria stands in the center.

PARCO DEI PRINCIPI
Added to the park in the
late nineteenth century,
this circular temple in the
classical style stands in
the midst of palm trees.
In front of the temple is
a bank of ferns and
agapanthus in full bloom.

ELISA LUCCHESI'S GARDEN

This very attractive and well cared for garden is distinguished by its imitation of the old intimate Sorrentino pattern of gardens. The essential elements are enclosed; tufa walls, bamboo windbreaks, citrus and other fruit trees, aromatic herbs, and rare flowers.

An ancient species of the highly perfumed pink centifolia rose on a bed of blue lobelia.

OPPOSITE: A bush of red Colombina roses with yellow hearts stands in the middle of the lawn in front of a palm tree.

NEXT PAGE: The tufa brick walls of the orchard surround lemon trees bordered by pelargonium Sorrentino, recognizable by its black heart. A medlar tree stands next to a tool shed covered by Ace of Hearts red climbing roses and on the right side Harry, a yellow rose.

116

HOTEL VITTORIA

High over the Marina Piccola, a playful agglomeration of buildings rises within an orange orchard, offering its guests a peaceful and verdant retreat overlooking the sea. Originally it consisted of four very different buildings: an aristocratic residence, a châlet, an old farmhouse and a fascinating turquoise conservatory decorated with wooden grillage, baskets of flowers and palmettos. The garden, filled with hidden statues, is planted with oranges, lemons, palms, hibiscus, bougainvillea and many other plants with Mediterranean perfumes and colors. An engaging art nouveau tea house with whimsical tile murals of trailing wisteria forms part of the terrace and is one of the best known sights of Sorrento.

The hotel entrance is through a wrought iron gate from the main town square. On the gate's left side a long wooden trellis supports wisteria and acts as a canopy for a pathway with a view on the sea. The main path leading to the hotel is bordered with carefully manicured flower beds planted in an assortment of intricate geometric patterns.

The Excelsior Vittoria is one of the oldest hotels in Italy. Over the centuries it has received visits from half of Europe's crowned heads, and has hosted the likes of Byron, Goethe, Wagner, and Verdi as well. The most requested suite today is the one named for Enrico Caruso, who spent many months at the Vittoria.

Bust on the railing of the terrace.

OPPOSITE: A trellis hung with wisteria shades a path leading to a view of the Mediterranean and the port with its fishing boats.

VILLA VITTORIA
The main stair leading to the hotel. Date and other palm trees growing in large pots and flowering clivia border the stone balustrade.

Detail of the art nouveau tea house with its painted tiles depicting trailing wisteria. This vine grows abundantly in Sorrento and the air is redolent with its perfume in springtime.

Museo Correale
Di Terranova

The Museo Correale di Terranova was created by Alfredo and Pompeo Correale, two refined connoisseurs of the arts who requested in their wills that the family villa, known as the Villa alla Rota, be transformed into a museum. The contents of the villa as well as the surrounding orchards, citrus groves, and farm house, opened in 1924 to the public and has delighted visitors ever since. Considered the most beautiful provincial museum in Italy, the Correale collection is particularly well endowed with the paintings, decorative arts and porcelain of Naples. These pieces date from the seventeenth century to the twentieth. The museum also houses Greek and Roman archaeological finds. The disastrous earthquake of 1980 heavily damaged the site, but after nine years of extensive restoration the museum reopened.

At the entrance an ample archway leads through a beautiful iron gate into a vast semi-circular esplanade. From here a wide flight of stairs climbs three floors, passing by large arched windows that overlook the sea and citrus groves. Surrounded by rare camellia Japonica the esplanade opens on an allée of plane trees on one side and citrus groves on the other. The allée continues to the sprawling colorful nurseries. From here a path descends through an underpass carved into the tufa brick wall, then opens onto the gulf where the panorama embraces the entire arch of the Sorrento coast.

The white flowers of the brugmansia, also called angel's trumpet, at the entrance of the garden. Lush and tropical in appearance, these flowers perfume only at night.

MUSEO CORREALE
Arched windows give a
wide view on the gulf from
the main staircase,
designed by G. B. Mauclerio
in the nineteenth century.
The walls of the staircase
are decorated with plaques
commemorating events
and persons connected
with the history of Sorrento.

A bed of the pelargonium
Sorrentino.

An array of colorful plants.

A Roman ruin is a garden ornament.

**A watercolor by Pompeo Correale
(1829–1900), representing the
entrance to the museum.**

VILLA SAVARESE

This villa in Sant'Agnello, a residential area near Sorrento, belonged to the English writer and poet Mary Crawford at the beginning of the twentieth century. At that time, a colony of English intellectuals vacationed in Sorrento, where they planted and created gardens.

The villa is now owned by Maria Savarese who has recreated the garden using mostly local plants and incorporated part of the garden into the house through a magnificent winter pavilion.

A few old mulberry trees are reminiscent of the early nineteenth century, when this area enjoyed a brief period as a center of silk production. After the rise of other silk markets Sorrento could no longer compete and oranges were cultivated instead. Some were grafted with lemon trees. Citrus fruits have since become one of the most typical and profitable products of the region.

A section of the swimming pool and one part of the patio are shaded by an extended lemon arbor. The citrus trees grow against a high wall typical of Sorrento, covered by climbing grape vines supported by bamboo stalks. Indonesian style furniture, trays overflowing with lemons, and pots filled with pansies adorn the pool side.

VILLA SAVARESE
At the end of the pool a gazebo made of tall bamboo trees forming a spacious cabana. Next to it, a large camellia tree grows in front of palms and yucca.

A potted male cycad displays its flower in full-bloom.

VILLA MONDA

An intimate garden with an iron gate entrance through a shaded allée leads to several outdoor garden–rooms. The first, similar to a parlor, is planted with palms on a green lawn. A staircase leads to a welcoming and comfortable patio furnished with cozy seating arrangements around a fountain. A half enclosed veranda with potted plants and flower borders is used both for cooking and eating. Each of the these outdoor spaces connects directly to the villa through doors. At the end of the garden a grove thick with orange and lemon trees is planted to give a sense of perspective and continuity.

A view into the garden from a room decorated by Renzo Mongiardino and the owner, Luciana Pane Monda. The trompe l'oeil painting of white and pink climbing roses successfully unites the outdoors with the interior of the house. The rose motif on the walls is echoed in the furniture upholstery.

Balustrade of a staircase with baroque shell decoration. On the right is a cycad and a Buonapartea palm.

In the patio, a marble tub filled with papyrus supports a nineteenth–century fountain with a sculpted mask. Bamboo grows on both sides of the patio next to the curved wall.

OPPOSITE: A bird's–eye view of the garden with a date palm tree on the left, a young pair of male and female cycads and a coconut tree. On the right a bougainvillea trellis covers the entrance to the villa.

VILLA MONDA

The front patio, furnished with wicker furniture, is paved with pebbles arranged in geometric patterns alternating with slate paths. On the right are papyrus leaves and in the background cycads, yucca, and palm trees.

An ancient pink blooming wood peony with a cocos tree in the background.

OPPOSITE: View towards the garden dotted with palms and lemon trees laden with fruit. Potted clivia and cicadea can be seen in the fore–ground. A cariota branch on the left completes the picture.

VILLA SILVANA

One of the characteristic features of gardens along the Sorrentino escarpment is a formal garden by the entrance with ample plantings and shaded walkways leading to the villa. The dramatic vistas over the gulf are on the opposite side where terraces are laid out with statuary and potted plants resilient to heat and sea air. From the terrace of Villa Silvana a sequence of steep steps leads down to a wooden dock in the old port of Sorrento. The rocky incline is richly planted with pine, ash, olive, and fig trees, grape vines, vegetables and flowers. Countless stones of all sizes are overgrown with climbers.

At the dock the final group of stairs drops to sea level. The white classical balustrades are accentuated by plants in terracotta pots.

OPPOSITE: **View from the upper terrace of the villa on the Gulf of Naples.**

VILLA SILVANA
A columned archway covers part of the steps descending from the villa. The retaining walls are in tufa brick and decorated with masks and appliques that serve as planters.

OPPOSITE: One of the terraces jutting over the sea makes a delightful place for meals.

136

VILLA ROSA

This evocative *Belle Epoque* villa was constructed in 1906 by the famous film director Carmine Gallone. He had fallen in love with a villa on Lake Como and had it reproduced overlooking the sea in Sorrento. The fact that the villa is a copy of another residence built far away, and is thus completely different in architectural style from its Sorrentino neighbors, gives Villa Rosa a distinctive air. Gaetano Mascolo, a local architect and builder, worked closely with the mistress of the house on its renovation. Under her careful and knowledgeable guidance the villa's orchards and delicate vegetation are kept in impeccable order.

View of the front staircase, designed by Raimonda Gaetani, who also planned the gardens. The steps are flanked by two pairs of cycads. Clever landscaping of caneraris, groups of papyrus, and other trees give a deep sense of perspective.

OPPOSITE: **This elegant flight of marble steps curves its way to the columned portico of the villa. A cedar of Lebanon bough over-hangs the area. Fern fronds can be seen peeping between the columns supporting the balustrade upon which stand two potted asparagus ferns.**

Detail of a protected corner of the garden.

VILLA ROSA

OPPOSITE AND ABOVE: **In the side garden a pergola constructed on two levels covers a pathway. This leads to a fountain encircled with flowering clivia, and crowned with a terracotta figure of Flora. The path itself is made of stone and is edged with agapanthus. The intoxicating perfume of innumerable gardenias and lemons spreads throughout this garden.**

RIGHT: **An elevated terrace decorated with terracotta figures that stand in front of the ubiquitous bamboo windbreak. This structure protects the pots of young cycads and other plants grown here and transplanted when they are mature.**

VILLA ASTOR

OPPOSITE: A view of the entrance to the villa.

The Villa Astor is reached by a narrow winding path flanked by high stone walls. Its imposing façade overlooks the gulf in solitary splendor, and this privileged location makes it one of the most spectacular sites in the area. The villa's history reaches back to Roman times. Once a convent of the order of Sta. Chiara stood on the property, but this was destroyed in 1558 by the Saracen hordes lead by Piali Pasha. Dominican monks took over the property and rebuilt the monastery. In 1888 the land and monastery were acquired by Baron Giovanni Labonia from Calabria, who built the present villa and adapted the gardens to include his important collection of archaeological finds.

During Labonia's tenancy, it was discovered that the villa was built on foundations laid by Agrippa Postumo, grandson of the Emperor Augustus. In the sea below the villa, some still water ponds are still in existence, testifying to the ancient practice of rearing moray eels.

By the turn-of-the-century Sorrento had become a fashionable watering place for men of letters as well as the *beau monde.* It attracted writers such as Henrik Ibsen, who wrote his masterpiece *Ghosts* here, and Maxim Gorki visited on his Italian tour. Richard Wagner was inspired to write the first act of *Parsifal* here, and Heinrich Schliemann, the discoverer of Troy and the controversial Treasure of Priam, was also a noted admirer of Sorrento and a guest of Baron Labonia.

During World War II Benedetto Croce fled from the Allied bombardments of Naples to the villa Astor and wrote his famous treatise *When Italy was Divided in Two* while overlooking the transparent waters of the gulf. Here Croce also had important conversations with King Umberto of Savoia, Harold Macmillan (later Prime Minister of Britain), Andre Wyschinsky (later Russian Minister of Foreign Affairs), Enrico De Nicola (first President of the Italian Republic) and many other politicians and scholars.

In 1905 Lord William Waldorf Astor, of American origin, bought a nearby property, sight unseen, in order to enlarge the garden of the Villa Labonia which he already owned.

Once both the gardens were combined within his property,
Lord Astor unscrupulously pulled down the former
Dominican monastery itself.

Renovations of the house and garden reflect the extrava-
gant and romantic tastes of the early 1900's, and inspired
Lord Astor to transform the gardens into a treasure–trove of

archaeological finds. Fountains, lakes, grottoes, niches, wells, and remains of former civilizations are interspersed with tropical plants, vines, countless varieties of palms, yuccas, Chamerops, and native plants and flowers. The result is a flourishing garden that is at once tranquil and richly exotic.

Lord Astor died in 1919 leaving Villa Astor as his legacy. Today, the villa and its garden remain one of the most important examples of English exoticism combined with native Italian tradition. The present owners, Rita and Mariano Pane, have devotedly maintained the garden in the spirit in which it was originally laid out by adding new trees and preserving the rare species already planted. In the words of the owner, "The beauty of this garden consists mainly in its age carried with great grace and dignity".

VILLA ASTOR
The Gothic well stands out amidst cycads and luxuriant vegetation.

OPPOSITE: An imposing statue of Neptune on a fluted pedestal surveys the waterlily pond. A trailer of wisteria appears in front; large yucca and palms grow in the background.

A head of Mars on a plinth by a shield of dry palm fronds. This construction is common to the area, and is used to protect plants during the rare cold days and to shade them from the wind and the hot summer sun.

146

The pavilion, on a spur overlooking the sea, displays a splendid panorama of the gulf. The heads of Minerva and Dionysus, and Zeus in the corner followed by Hera and Mars, were carved by Laurens Alma Tadema in the nineteenth century. Created expressly for Lord Astor, they exemplify the love for classicism typical of the time.

VILLA ASTOR

OPPOSITE: The stone well was the center of the monastery originally located here and retains its antique iron work. Next to it stands a phoenix dactylifera palm and in front, a papyrus.

An amphora covered by a Ficus repens.

An Early Christian sarcophagus stands at the end of the garden in a shed built with the so–called *opus reticulatum* technique. The book in their hands shows that the couple were literate and from a privileged class.

On the left a Japanese kumquat with its orange fruit grows on the lawn while on the other side of the path a large Washingtonia stands over a Nolina pincenectia. An aloe, an agave, a large yucca, an olive tree and a dactolifera can also be seen.

A blue agapanthus flower.

A Roman bifurcate window frames a panorama of the gulf. Although the garden is on a terrace overlooking the sea, Lord Astor had a wall pierced with small windows built along it. An allée covered by Aeleagnus pungens and yellow Banksiea roses parallels the wall and makes this path one of the most romantic and panoramic walks in this garden.

VILLA ASTOR

OPPOSITE: An allée of Chamaedoreae elegans leads to a Baroque fountain decorated with lion heads and a crest displaying a rampant griffin. Palms grow in large terracotta pots and a spread of orange clivia borders the stone path. The trellis is covered with white Banksiea roses.

In one of the green lawns in the midst of this Alice in Wonderland tropical garden, a magic table appears. The delicacies on it have all been prepared and cooked with the products of the vegetable garden.

MASSA LUBRENSE

The small garden is thickly planted with a lemon grove, which provides a cool, green retreat from the blinding light of the sea.

At one time, Massa Lubrense was an agricultural center as well as a fishing village. Among its products were lemons, prized for their small size and unusually thin rinds, which were put to particularly good use in *Limoncello*, the local liqueur. It has since become a vacation spot with homes and pocket-sized gardens descending gently to the harbour. The island of Capri provides a beautiful backdrop.

OPPOSITE: View through a vine covered archway on the terrace looking into the lemon grove. An amphora on the ground holds cut hydrangeas while an asparagus fern trails over the old terracotta floor.

MASSA LUBRENSE
OPPOSITE: A terrace with potted plants looking over the sea at sunset.

Raised flower boxes stand in front of a wall.

Clivia borders a garden path.

VILLA SANT'AGATA

A trailer of rare, white Concord grape vine extends from the pergola that shades a corner of the garden with its masses of fuchsia and coffee-house style wrought iron furniture.

OPPOSITE: The hand-made wrought iron entrance gate is complemented by light mauve hydrangeas which abound in the climate of the peninsula. A verdant hazelnut tree stands in the background.

Situated eight hundred meters above sea level between the Gulf of Naples and the Gulf of Salerno, Villa Sant'Agata was once a famous functioning farm producing hazel nuts, chestnuts and apples, as well as milk from its large dairy operation. Its altitude precludes the cultivation of citrus fruits, which abound in the plains below. Today, traversed by numerous roads, the property is only a fraction of the size it once was. Signora Rosa Pane Cuomo, granddaughter of the original owner, has made a life–long commitment to keep the land in pristine condition and has transformed the acreage into an impressive fruit and vegetable garden-farm. The aura of the past is sustained by employing a number of techniques used in former days as well as present day technology.

Gardens brimming with flowers alternate with plots devoted to eggplant, rare pink tomatoes, peppers of all colors, broad beans, artichokes, and sweet white onions. Pergolas heavy with delicious and rare table grapes are located throughout the property, as well as prune, apple, pear, fig and quince, persimmon and a few scattered olive trees. Hedges of raspberries as well as plots of strawberries are also to be found in this carefully tended vegetable and fruit farm.

The garden is also planted with fruit trees growing on the green lawn, along with climbers of wisteria, clematis, jasmine, and other vines which grow tenaciously over the walls and along the many pergolas, trellises, and covered pathways.

It is one of the few places where species of fruits and vegetables near extinction are carefully maintained and new varieties are regularly introduced .

VILLA SANT'AGATA

An immense lawn extends from the villa's living-room to the fruit orchard. A large marquee of striped canvas, hand-tied to its supports, serves as an open-air extension of the living room. The pillows of the wicker chairs are covered with antique embroidery.

Allée leading to the fruit orchards and vegetable gardens. The clusters of bright green table grapes are protected by their leaves from the rays of the hot sun.

NEXT PAGE: A curved, moss-covered old stone bench overhung with camellia branches in full-bloom.

AMALFI COAST

Winding through hills covered with olive trees, groves of citrus trees, the Amalfi coast road passes through many towns and villages. Most of these are built on steep hills with wild precipices and cut by steep flights of steps. This road is famous for its dramatic views of the ocean, which is constantly visible far below. The gardens are laid out on terraces, courtyards and small plots of land. Many kinds of Mediterranean plants and bushes creep between the stone walls that flank the streets and in the gorges of the mountains. Numerous carob trees, prickly pears and all sorts of scented herbs spring out of crevices and intermingle with yellow broom and caper bushes with their white and lilac flowers. Every window bursts with flowers growing in lush and colorful profusion.

View from the Le Sirenuse in Positano on the intricately tiled roof of the church. The many small terraced gardens of the village are also visible. Roses and other seasonal flowering plants accentuate the sun-bleached whiteness of the stucco wall.

165

POSITANO

Located off a narrow street, a huge doorway leads to the large inner court of the Moorish–style Murat palace which has now been transformed into a hotel.

OPPOSITE: A climbing rose adorns a column on a terrace. A bench decorated with local Salerno tiles from which Positano and the endless expanse of the sea can be seen.

POSITANO: LE SIRENUSE

Le Sirenuse gets much of its charm from its enchanting position overlooking the Tirrenian sea, with the Isles of the Sirens floating in the near distance. Ulysses is said to have passed by these islands, and to avoid succumbing to the sirens's blandishments, he stuffed the sailors' ears and had himself bound to the mast of his ship. The family of the present owners of the hotel, the Sersales, once owned all these islands. Originally the hotel, with its lovely terraces and small plots for floral and vegetable gardens, was their home. Today the garden's bounty is used in the renowned hotel kitchen, whose secrets are now taught in the family's school of traditional Neapolitan cooking. In 1951 the family turned the villa into a six room hotel which has grown into one of the most sought after resorts in Italy. The terraces have grown, along with the hotel, both in number and size. A myriad of plantings can be found throughout the hotel and around the pool, as well as on the many terraces and balconies. These reflect great attention to detail, and are lov-ingly cared for and changed with each season to provide a bright and colorful view.

As seen from the balcony of the hotel, the main terrace overlooking the sea is enriched by potted plants. Luxurious bougainvillea climb over the trellis and potted begonias and hibiscus are used as decoration. The yellow alamanda flowers contrast with the white edge of the terrace and seem to grow directly from the sea.

Detail of an antique hand-painted basin recessed in a brightly painted stucco wall.

LE SIRENUSE

On one of the smaller terraces, a white balustrade stands out against the red walls, while a profusion of geranium spills out of a pot. Red and orange hibiscus, rosemary, roses, potted pomegranates and the omnipresent bougain-villea are scattered all over.

OPPOSITE: The swimming pool, designed by Fausta Gaetani and Patrizia Ruspoli, is bordered by lemon trees. These are planted in ornate terracotta planters standing on white bases decorated with a wave-like motif. At the end of the pool, a beautiful mosaic depicts frolicking mermaids.

Tre Ville,
Arienso

This lovely estate once held three villas that have now been combined into one residence. The remains of a wooden dancing platform, an unusual item in Positano, are still in evidence, attesting to the presence here of either Nijinsky or Leonide Massine. Both spent time in the area before the present owner, Maestro Franco Zeffirelli, acquired the property. The Maestro cherishes his gardens and returns with plants and seeds from all his worldwide travels. These are transplanted faithfully and successfully in every corner of the property.

Years ago when the many gardens were destroyed by a tidal wave in Sorrento, huge trees and other smaller vegetation were hurled into the sea. Zeffirelli and his neighbor took it upon themselves to salvage boatloads of these plants. They transported them to Positano and used them to create a botanical garden, saving the plants from disappearing forever.

In different parts of the garden, Zeffirelli has followed the charming custom, dating back to Roman times, of interspersing small groups of aromatic herbs among the other plantings. Parsley, basil, sage, mint, and rosemary fill the air with their beguiling fragrance and attract the attention of countless butterflies.

Maestro Zeffirelli welcoms many of his colleagues and world–famous friends at his villa. Guests are provided with every convenience, and the garden offers the one most prized: privacy. The shaded terraces, each on a separate level, are perfect for relaxing and are built along the rocks throughout the garden.

From the sea, the white–washed villa stands out clearly while the many terraced gardens which surround it can only be glimpsed. The gardens abound with many varieties of flowers, vines and multi-colored climbers, as well as a few vegetable beds kept as they were in the past. The terraces are connected by paths and stone steps to each other and to the different levels of the villa. The undulating terrain creates interesting contrasts of sun and shade.

TRE VILLE

OPPOSITE: **An oleander branch fights its way through the wisteria pergola that covers the terrace. Green painted wicker furniture and a stone bench bordering the area provide seating.**

Steps lead to a Moorish–style tiled archway, one of the entrances to the villa. A Monstera vine climbs against the pink stucco wall.

TRE VILLE

OPPOSITE: A bougainvillea adorns one of the brick–paved pathways leading from the main terrace. These pathways and numerous stairs lead from one terrace to another and connect the surrounding terraces to various parts of the garden. Many of them have breathtaking views of the sea. The climbing bougainvillea here springs from a local amphora.

One of the terraces that offers stunning views of Positano. Blue agapanthus growing in pots are mixed with evergreens. Yuccas can be seen in the background.

TRE VILLE
Water reaches the garden
from a spring in the
mountain overlooking the
villa and trickles down the
mossy stone channel.

The entrance to the villa is located off the main square of
Ravello, through an imposing archway in a medieval tower
shaded by a majestic cypress. An allée bordered with trees
leads to different parts of the garden. The villa itself is now
the home of the Center for Research for Villas and their
Urban Environments, and the garden serves as a perfect set-
ting for the many concerts given here during the summer.

On the right of the villa stands the famous Moorish
cloister. On the left the Torre Maggiore looms over the top
garden with its many colorful round flower–beds. From the
tower the splendid lower garden appears, culminating in the
bright colors of the celebrated belvedere, which presents one
of the best-known views of the coast. The rectangular prom–
enade that stretches along the garden is planted with geo–
metric flower–beds, with palms growing from the center of
some of them. A fountain serves as the centerpiece to this
parterre. The play of light on sea and sky further heightens
the charm of this evocative vista.

VILLA RUFOLO
A view of the length of the parterre with pink geranium in terracotta planters on the balustrade.

The columned terrace rises above permanent stone beds planted throughout the year to reflect the passing seasons.

OPPOSITE: Intense scarlet sage blossoms highlight the greenery bordering the columned walk with its view over the mountains.

186

VILLA RUFOLO
Views through the arches. The left wall of the courtyard is covered by bougainvillea, while at the right flower beds are planted with multi–colored pansies. The courtyard, lined with double loggias in the Moorish–style, is reached from the parterre through romantic hidden stairs overgrown with vines and decorated with potted plants. The garden loggia, a reminder of the pleasure–garden architecture of the thirteenth century, was probably designed to function as an outdoor dining room with painted arches open to the sea breeze.

VILLA RUFOLO
The rose pergola stands out against the intense blue sky of the Amalfi coastline. The tapered tops of cypress trees can be seen growing on a lower terrace.

OPPOSITE: a detail of the cloister with its Moorish decoration.

VILLA CIMBRONE

The land upon which the present Villa Cimbrone stands belonged, among others, to the Accongiagoco family. It was purchased in 1904 by the wealthy English banker, Lord Grimthorpe, an expert on horology who designed Big Ben. He bought a large area of hillside, a magnificent site with endless views of the sea. Lord Grimthorpe enlisted the services of Niccoló Mansi to create the garden and, at the same time, help him place his countless pieces of sculpture copying classic, medieval and Renaissance originals.

Together, Grimthorpe and Mansi created an inventive, varied, and eccentric garden layout combining English tradition with Italian design. Its English flavor is partially due to its complex arrangement of panoramic views and the variations of perspectives and colors that characterize the garden at villa Cimbrone. Lord Grimthorpe's knowledge of classical art and architecture accounts for the decorative details and inscriptions abounding in the garden. These small touches serve to enhance the sculptures interspersed among the plantings throughout the park.

On the left side of the entrance to the garden stands a fourteenth-century style cloister with a covered central well built in 1917. Next to this stands the main building, which over the years hosted many well-known visitors, among them Greta Garbo and Leopold Stokowski. From here a long straight allée of 500 meters flanked by columns, pots, and plinths, divides the property. This extraordinary approach leads to a circular temple where the goddess Ceres protects the area from underneath her domed glorietta. Her promise of fertility and plenty seems echoed in the expanse of sea and infinite greenery. From here extends the belvedere, dotted with eighteenth-century busts of emperors along the railing. This clifftop, 350 meters above sea, juts out and offers an unobstructed view of both sides of the Amalfi coast.

VILLA CIMBRONE

Multi-colored flowers are planted in beds with terracotta edging in front of the neo–Byzantine pavilion, the preferred spot for Lord Grimthorpe to drink tea. In front of the pavilion extends a formally planted and laid–out parterre filled with reproductions of statuary from Pompeii and other places.

OPPOSITE: Detail of a corner of the pavilion showing its Moorish–tiled archway.

NEXT PAGE:

By the rose garden an immense urn on a marble base backed by umbrella pines and gray limestone dominates the cloudless sky.

Columns made of sun–baked brick support a trellis of Banksiae roses. The well in front is protected by an elaborate wrought iron cover and is sheltered by an umbrella pine.

VILLA CIMBRONE

The western side of the garden is reached through rock gardens,
grottoes, arcades, clipped hedges, and various fanciful follies.
A bronze statue of an athlete is situated on a panoramic walk,
an enchanting spot from which to admire the view of the sea.

OPPOSITE: Cypress flank the allée
leading to the temple of Bacchus.
This structure of eight classical
columns protects the god and houses
the ashes of Lord Grimthorpe.

A copy of Donatello's David and
Goliath stands on a stone pedestal
and is enclosed by clipped box
hedges.

A copy of a Greek statue surrounded
by blooming hydrangea ornaments
the main axis of the garden. A
border of agapanthus can be seen in
the background.

VILLA CIMBRONE
Attached to the circular temple is the famous belvedere terrace,
elevated 300 meters above the sea. This noble area is adorned with
eighteenth century busts.

VILLA CIMBRONE
The Moorish courtyard by
the entrance to the villa.

LA RONDINAIA

In 1925 Lord Grimthorpe's daughter built a villa on the western slope of Villa Cimbrone, her father's estate. The entrance to the villa, through a small gate on a side road off the main square in Ravello, leads to lovely paths that hug the steep hillside and offer panoramic views towards the villages of Maiori and Minori. The present owner, inspired by local gardening traditions, has embellished his hillside property with perennials and trees in harmony with the environment of the site. The combination of the steep slope to the sea on one side, and the escarpment rising above it lends La Rondinaia an atmosphere of complete privacy.

OPPOSITE: **The villa end its surrounding rocky garden, accessible through terraces and a winding path, seen from a pergola crowned with clusters of wisteria.**

Beds of blue iris thrive throughout the garden.

LA RONDINAIA

The pool, lined with lapis lazuli colored tiles, lies
below an allée of cypress and clipped hedges.

OPPOSITE: A pathway bordered by cypress opens a
view to the sea that can be reached by a sequence
of steep steps.

LA RONDINAIA
Detail of the path to the
villa showing the trunk of
an olive tree and one of the
many natural grottoes in
the rock.

Detail of the flowers
growing along the side of
the path.

OPPOSITE: The path to the
villa along the hillside is
lined with geranium, iris,
lily, aquileia, snap–dragon
and other plants which
thrive in the rocky terrain.

PAESTUM

S outh of the River Sele, close by the sea, the famous Greek
temples of Paestum appear gleaming in the sunlight.

Founded as a Sybarite colony in 600 B.C. and called
Poseidonia for the god of the sea, it became a flourishing
town by 540 B.C. Before being subdued by the Romans and
absorbed into the Empire as a colony, Paestum was besieged
by the notoriously bellicose Lucani. From the ninth to the
nineteenth century the area, which is surrounded by forests
and malarial swamps, was deserted.

Paestum has become one of the principal sites of archaeological interest in Italy. The former marshes were transformed
into fertile fields as well as almond and citrus orchards. Herds
of sheep, cattle and buffalo (Goethe remarks on these animals
in his *Italian Journey* in 1787, likening them to hippopotamus)
graze in the lush grassland.

A flowering apple tree
grows by the ruins of the
Temple of Peace.

OPPOSITE: Doric temple
dedicated to Ceres, built in
the sixth century B.C. Next
to it grows a Judas tree
with its delicate mauve
early spring flowers.

INDEX